MW01178658

HEART-BEAT

MIRNA S. ISKANDAR

ISBN: 978-0-9959168-0-7

Book Cover by: Eddie Dagher

DEAR READER,

Thank you for choosing to read my book.

As you read through the pages of this poetry book, I hope you capture the emotions and feelings that inspired some of these poems. The Journey of your life will sometimes feel like a rollercoaster with many ups and downs, where you might end up facing a crossroad and it is up to you to choose which path you want to take.

My wish for you is to learn from the lessons that fashioned few of these experiences, as such you will be able to make better choices in your life path. I hope to inspire you to live with love, kindness, and passion.

Remember, you always have a choice and never forget that your conscience and your heart are what keep you human.

THANK YOU,

MIRNA S. ISKANDAR

ACKNOWLEDGMENT

I would like to thank God for blessing me with such a gift and talent, for allowing me to use it, and for always guiding my path

My family, in particular, my parents, who were instrumental in my upbringing. They were always there for me no matter what life threw in my path. Their encouragement, patience, and dedication helped me become the person I am today

My brother, Sami, for always pushing me to strive beyond my limits and always inspiring me

My close friend, Kerian, for pushing me to save my poems and publish them. It was an extremely hard decision

Finally, a thank you for all the family, friends and life in general for influencing me one way or another be it by being my muse or inspiring these myriads of feelings that resonated into these poems.

DEDICATION

To my Family

CONTENTS

THE JOURNEY

MIRNA S. ISKANDAR

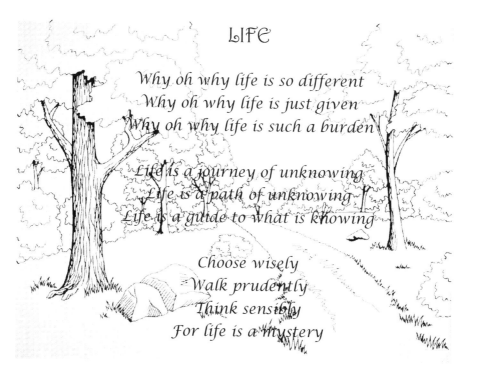

LIFE

Why oh why life is so different
Why oh why life is just given
Why oh why life is such a burden

Life is a journey of unknowing
Life is a path of unknowing
Life is a guide to what is knowing

Choose wisely
Walk prudently
Think sensibly
For life is a mystery

JOURNEY

Life is short yet fulfilling
Life is a mystery yet amazing
Life is a puzzle yet well knowing

Life is nothing but a story
A story of emotions
Life is nothing but a journey
A journey of reactions

The love that fills your heart
Your being and your soul
Where eyes see nothing but a smile
Where the soul is filled with excitement
Where the world is good and breathtaking
Where life becomes worth living

The happiness that takes your being
Filling your heart with love and passion
Where eyes lusting and desiring
Where the soul flutters in expectation
Where the world is optimistic and abiding
Where life becomes worth dying

The disappointment that moves your being
Takes over you and your existence
Where eyes filled with disbelieving
Where the soul aches in its grievance
Where the world is wrong and in disgrace
Where life becomes the least choice

The hurt that strikes through the heart
Makes you bleed with no remedy
Where eyes see nothing but torment
Where the soul is nearing expiry
Where the world is dark and anguishing
Where life becomes not worth living

IS RELIEF HERE

Walking around
Looking around
Crowded spaces
Questioning faces
Looking at me
Questioning me
Is relief here

Starving bodies
Pale as zombies
Waiting for relief
From all this mischief
Asking and wondering
Praying and hoping
Is relief here

One will have pity
On this great city
Full of ecstasy
Yet,
Dying from poverty
Food- is scarce
Shelter- is sparse
Is relief here

Children yearning
For comfort touching
To sooth their soul
Their mind console
Is relief here

Houses with acres
Huge, massive spaces
Those in power housing,
Slums and shelters
Crowding and masses
Those in dire hiding,
Is relief here

Why oh why
Such a big discrepancies
In one and all these cities,
Rich or poor
No middle in the pool,
Society accepting
This gap increasing
As the rich one investing
And the poor one delivering
Is relief here

DO I ???

A walk on this land
A journey on this earth
How long is it?
What is it for?
Why am I here?
When will I know?

Do I wonder aimlessly?
Do I care about anything?
Do I care about anyone?
How do I know thee?
Do I dare dream?
Do I give my heart away?
Do I love thee?

What would I get in return?
Do I gamble on what I will get?
Do I get the same?
Will you protect my heart?
Will you care for it?
Do I trust thee?

WHAT CONSCIOUS!

An eye for an eye, A tooth for a tooth
All around us, That's the world we liveth
A brother against a brother
A son against a father
As the son defies the father
That's where we are

A distant memory, Of a forgotten world
So sl-ow-ly erased, As a blind eye is turned:
To the homeless men
To the starving children
To the abused women
To the murdered human
To the genocide of a faith

Long gone the conscious away
The one that showed us the way
The one that kept humanity
To live in peace and harmony:
How to be kind
How to be concerned
How to be giving
How to be loving
How to be human

Gone are the days of innocence
Laws based on harmony and peace
Where the laws of humanity spread
Continent to continent and beyond:
Respecting each other
Protecting each other
Believing in each other
Providing and sharing
But most importantly
Caring and loving

All the goodness- vanished
All of humanity- stripped
As new laws took over-eth
The laws of this earth:
Stealing and cheating
Abusing and killing
Lusting and sinning
Greed and power
But most importantly
Using each other

Living from moment to moment
No consequences, no punishment
Without a care in the world
No cost except- killing our breed
Only getting stronger and stronger
With more and more power
Becoming less of a human
And more of- a monument.

MY COUNTRY

My country oh my country
Full of magic and beauty
From up above was given
To this land of haven
To blossom and be nurtured
To be plentiful and treasured

Greenery that fills the air
For all humanity to share,
From the slopes filled with snow
White fluff- to never plow,
To the sandy beaches for all to see
Leaving others filled with envy

The sun that shines all its rays
On this land that is a maze,
It is a wonder from the higher
With a mystical desire

But alas lost in confusion
From one and all its direction,
Governed by those in power
Filled with undeserving power

Full of corruption and desire
Thinking they are the higher
For greed is their intention
And consciousness for destruction,

Eternal life- they seek
Endless power- they need
Left and right killing and stealing
Clear and obvious bribing and destroying

What was once filled with shades
It is now full of blades,
What was once a safety haven
It is now a place that threaten,
What was once a heaven
Nothing was left but a hell-in

Yee oh yee of little faith
Creating havoc on this earth,
Eternity- will never be
You're never deserving of thee

For the almighty is here
He will find you far and near,
To give judgment of all your deeds
To heal the soul of all who bleeds,
For my country is a beauty
From the ONE and MIGHTY.

WONDER WONDER

Flake by flake
They fall from the sky,
One by one
They form a bundle,
White like the purest of the hearts
Soft like a ball of cotton
Yet,
They easily melt away
Like they never existed,
Disappearing
As fast as they arrived,
Disappearing
into nothingness

Alas,
They keep us wondering,
Would the next one be the same
Would I find the exact same one
One will never know
For it is all- a mystery

GRATEFUL FOR IT ALL

Taking a stroll in the wilderness
Absorbing all its freshness,
A long drive with no end in sight
A freeing feeling with a powerful might
A glimpse, of breathtaking scenery
All around filled with greenery,
Colors-as varied as the existence on this land
Trees-as mystical as a magical wand

Majestic trees higher and higher keeps aiming
Leaves flying and whispering sweet nothing,
Without a care in the world- the birds flying
Like no other exist- twittering and singing;
As the enchanting music starts playing
And all its notes- start dancing

Soft lips - lightly touching
As the lyrics try seeping,
A breeze - gently caressing
The cheeks of a free being,
Their existence announcing
With every sound participating
With the view entering
With the birds racing
With the music competing

The blue sky within an arm's reach
Seeking the attention- of each,
As the sun sends its warmth
All over this existing earth
Open space- with no walls around
Hair- freely flying all around
Accessing all available freshness
Beaming from this majestic wilderness

The view as vast as the eye can reach:
Taking in the scenery with every stretch
Taking in the fresh air with every inhalation
Taking in the flying birds with every
reverberation
Taking in the sunshine with every sense
Taking in the sky with every glance,

Being grateful- for it all

FAITH

TEMPTATION

On this earth- we all wonder
To learn, grow, and discover,
They say- stay true to yourself
But no one knows who is- the self

Earth is nothing but a journey
Until we make it to eternity,
What is eternity I inquire
How and when do we get there

The key to eternity is to exist
With pure soul, mind, and heart,
There must be a trick to it all
For this journey- of sin is plentiful:

Corrupting and Bribing
Robbing and Stealing
Fibbing and Lying
Slaying and Killing

Yearning and Desiring
Lusting and Pleasuring
Conniving and Gossiping
Deceiving and Cheating

How is one to trounce
The feeling of indulgence
It controls, takes over your being
It consumes, conquers your feeling

Turning and spiraling in all direction
Looking for answers in many direction
Kneeling, praying, and asking
An answer demanding and requesting

Lots of promises were made
From the bible they were heard,
Change your ways and repent
So that Jesus- your soul mend

In belief - one must be robust
In faith - one must be resilient
To fight it - one must find a way
To win - one must walk away

For one to gain recognition
Give love to all creation
Live in peace and harmony
To receive love- in eternity

LOST

Born in a place where the sacred remain
Praying and feeling the wholly within,
Dedicating oneself to live the life
That is acceptable to the ONE

A shock to the system that sends a shiver
Resets all what was known and believed
Rethinking all that was learned
Revolting and discovering other

Discovering the feeling of ecstasy
The emotions that fills all your being
Exploring more and experimenting
Lost in the wonder of this ecstasy

Realizing then what was done
Betraying yourself and your belief
Filled with regrets and plenty of grief
How far from the sacred you have gone

A broken heart and a shattered mind
Start wondering what has changed
Leaving the life that was once believed
To another that was not valid

Try as I might to go back in time
To figure out what has changed
To lead someone to a stray road
Fullspeedahead still forging- was time

Unable to stop such grave realization
A shameful feeling fills one's existence,
Tears streaming with unstoppable vengeance
Damning it all- and especially this nation

A flamed torch- the inside is burning
For the fire of regrets has taken over
The mind and the soul are both on fire
Yelling and screaming- the ONE is hurting.

DESPAIR

When the world is dark, no light in sight
Nowhere to run and nowhere to hide
What can I do and where can I go
Wanting to run away but unable to go

When everything you do and say is wrong
Greatly wanting to fix what went wrong
But only managed to do the same
Unintentional- yet still the same

Screaming, yelling, and crying
An answer asking and requesting
This pain filling and crowding the inside
Hoping for an answer- to find

Throw myself at the feet of the merciful
Knowing that HIS forgiveness is plentiful
Wishing for a quick, deep relief to appear
Praying for a forgiveness to transpire

Full of shame and confusion
Unable to allow the face an elevation
Instead kneeling and pleading
All that was lost reciting

Lost in my thoughts of misery
Losing the grasp of reality
For a new path begging
A new start to allow the healing

From the guilt, the soul exhausted
From the pleading, the body ached
The spirit giving up slowly
The mind shutting down slowly

Hopelessly gathering myself
From the ground pulling oneself
Trying to make it home again
Dragging - until home again

Giving up everything, the body throwing
Forgetting everything, the eyes Shutting
Hoping for a deeper sleep to fall
That would allow one to forget it all.

THE END

Living in this world
Without a care or worried
Taking and enjoying
Lusting and pleasing
Flesh and body celebrating
Both fully satisfying

Forgetting and not thinking
About the nearest ending:
What would transpire
When is this all over,
When the last breath is done,
When the last deed is done,
And the flesh goes down
And the soul - It is unknown

How frail are humans
To ignore all the signs
Only to face what has been always known
Fears and sorrows will forever be known

In this life and the following
Keep hunting and chasing
Until we repent - and give it our all
That is when - we will gain it all

So repent, repent, repent
For this life to amend,
For the lord is merciful
And always plentiful,
With his mercy and kindness
He will grant you forgiveness,
To your final destination
He will grant you admission

NOW IS THE TIME

Your life is a gift, Don't waste it
Your journey is a chance, Don't ruin it
Walk the path, Righteous
Do what is, Arduous

The eyes - always seeing
The heart - still beating
The mind - curiously wondering
The will - continuously fighting
The desire - strongly pushing
To give it up - and start doing
The little inner voice - ignoring

Resist, resist, resist,
Time not yet lost,
Now, is the time to fight
Now, is the time to set it right
Now, is the time to fulfill your destiny
Now, is the time to claim eternity

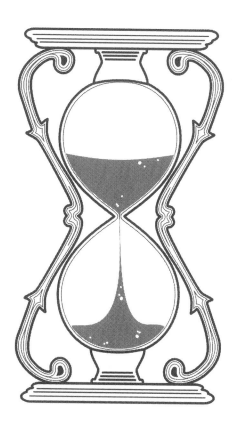

FORGIVENESS

Filled with emotions so anguished
Everlasting and intertwined,
Screaming, yelling, and crying
Trying to escape through running

For a peaceful being so fine
Find such enlightening divine,
Through the image of his creator
Kneels, pray, and ask for a favor

Lord of glory and forgiveness
Take my hand in full kindness,
Save me from my own doing
For I am weak and unknowing

Using his mighty hands and feet
HE pulls me straight to my feet,
Filling me with hope and delight
HE renders me strong and might

Forgiving- all of my deed
Asking me- to pray indeed
For life is nothing but a journey
To see who deserves ME - eternally

WHAT DO I NEED

The GOD of heaven-

Is all I need

For HE is the creator-

And the head

Of all that is real-

And that is eternal

HE is waiting

For your- Invitein

Open your hearts-

And let him in

For HE can give you-

All that you need

Pure heart,

And peaceful mind,

Unconditional love,

And eternal life.

HE is - the be all,

And end all

HEART-BEAT

33

MIRROR IMAGE

Look at the mirror...
Stand tall,
Feet- flat on the ground,
Shoulders erect,
Head straight ahead,
Look in front of you,
Straight ahead,
What do you see,
Do you see your reflection

Look in the mirror...
Look really deep,
Look at the details,
Look at the changes
Do you notice the changes,
Do you remember how they happened

Look at you in the mirror...
Is it still you,
Are you the same person,
Are you the one created into Jesus' image,
Do you still have the same morals,
Do you still have the same ethics,
Does humanity mean anything to you,
Do you give -
                Unconditionally,
Do you love -
                Unconditionally

34

Look through the mirror....
Are you ready,
Is your final dance finished,
Are you ready,
Is your legacy completed,
Are you ready,
How will you be remembered,
Are you ready,
Can you face your maker,
Are you ready?

FLOATING

Floating high

In mid air

Not on earth-

Yet

Not in the sky,

Admiring the view-

Yet

Unable to touch,

Imagining the feeling-

Yet

Unable to feel,

To bring it all in-

With a breathless sigh,

Wondering how-

The magnificent-

Did it all

DARKNESS OR LIGHT

Last deed completed,
Last word spoken,
Last breath taken,

Do I fear thee,
Do I trust thee,
Do I try to evade you,
Do I welcome you

Darkness or light, what would I see
Complete darkness would it be?
Filling the world we live in
Like a blind man wondering
Whereabouts would I be?

Fading away in every way
Into the shadows- fading away
All the colours near and far
All beings in this earth and far

Would it come knocking!
Would it be appearing!
Would it warn me!
Would it surprise me!

Would it recognize me!
Would it scare me!
Would I recognize it!
Would I welcome it!

Darkness or light- what would I see
That is the question- at the end of it all

LOOKING INTO YOUR EYES

Looking into your eyes,
What would I see,
How would I react

Looking into your eyes,
I am without a breath,
I am without consciousness

Looking into your eyes,
My eyes widened with a smile,
My pupils complete a full circle,
My cheeks climb high
For my lips to make a sigh,
Allowing my teeth to steal a sight
Filling them with all the light

Looking into your eyes,
Profoundly and with intent depth,
My heart skips- a beating breath,
My body shivers and wobble,
My legs shake and tremble

Filled with enjoyment and delight
My hands extend straight into the light,
Reaching out to touch the MIGHT
Though they disappear into the bright,
I do not panic nor frightened
For I know that I am blessed

Looking into your eyes,
Understanding the beginning of it all,
Recognizing- the meaning of it all

Looking into your eyes,
Light shining bright:
Full of happiness and delight
Full of warmth and tenderness
Providing hope and kindness

Looking into your eyes,
I see beauty at its finest

THE POWER THAT BE

The power that be created us
In his image and his spirit
Filled with love and purity
For each and every one of us

Love one another HE said
The way I do and always did,
From the heaven- I came for you
What love is- to show all of you

Giving up my eternity- was not enough
Becoming human- was not enough
Suffering and dying- was not enough
To convince you of what is- enough

Be the guidance for those lost
And shine oh so bright their path,
Bring them back to the right path
So they could be- no more lost

ALL I AM

All I am is a tool-
To do as you wish
and command,
Help me to stay the course-
And walk the path - You carved

All I am is a tool-
A weakling with a lesser power
Made up of human flesh and bones
Trying to resist what is presented here

All I am is a tool-
So use your wisdom-
And your strength
To keep me from - walking astray,
Use your forgiveness
And your loveth
To make me strong - And the course stay

YOU ARE

You are the eyes
        with which I see the world,

You are the breath
        that keeps me alive in this world,

You are the beat
        that keeps my heart pumping,

You are the light
        that keeps my path shining,

You are the smile
        that keeps my face lit up,

You are the joy
        that keeps my spirit up,

You are the rhythm
        that keeps music in the world,

You are the breeze
        that keeps me grounded,

You are my everything,
        You are my life

FRIENDSHIP

TRUST

A great big world

             with lots of weight on board

Full of surprises

             and lots of feelings involved

Trust- is the essence of all humanity
The one connection - we all seek - actually

A powerful emotion

             that weighs a lot,

So hard to earn

             yet too easily lost,

To trust someone - is to be free:
             To talk, to do, to be;
                         just free

BETRAYAL

Finding a dear friend is hard to do
Trusting someone is hard to do,
When trust becomes too innate
And friendship becomes to intimate,
Lines will be crossed
And boundaries erased

You think you found the one
But alas- think again my dear one

For disappointment will sure be yours
As the friend is nothing but a player
Disguised under the name of a friend
For a goal is set to be attained

Once his outcome is achieved
Nothing is left but to leave:
One is left satisfied
The other- crushed

For what was thought to be frank
Was found to be nothing but fake,
What was thought to be a supporter
Was found to be- a stranger

Using trust to make one fall
And get trapped in his wall,
Using flattery and charm as a weapon
To win the game with a touchdown

Who needs enemies anymore
When a friend can damage you more,
For a betrayal from a friend-lover
Is the worst kind of torture

A sharp knife through the heart
A stabbing- that is on repeat,
Injuring more than the heart
It is the soul that keeps the hurt

Trust shattered in all direction
Emotions flying in all direction
Trying to figure out the way
To make sense of what went array

But alas- no explanation is found
For a betrayal is the only one found,
Betrayal from a friend is one everlasting
The one that stays and never forgetting

The wound so deep and so entrenched
Eternal lesson was definitely learned,
Those who speak with tendering
Many compliments freely giving

Their web of lies spreading around
With the aim to catch honey round,
Run away from such one who lied
As to avoid- getting fried.

FRIEND OR FOE, WHAT ARE YOU

Try as I might to run away
The body unable to move away,
For the tension between us-
Closer and closer pulling us

The body stopped fighting
The will started shining,
For tonight is the night
Where the two unite

Inching closer and closer together
Unable to resist this power,
Two bodies into one
In a perfect intertwine

Ahh with this magical release
From the tension finding relief
For this tension not letting loose
Begging- for more and more release

A friend or foe- tell me please
When the moon disappears
And the sun is here,
Will I find you near
Or similar to the moon- you disappear

Friend or Foe, What are you

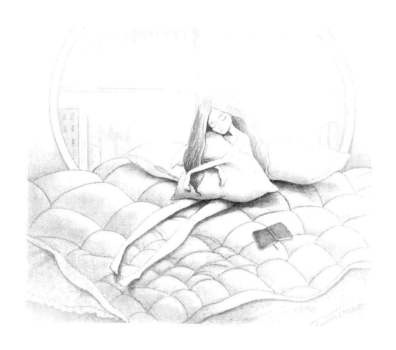

A FRIEND OR A LOVER

A friend or a lover- what will it be
The look - that gives chills all over me
For the tension is so great
An intention must be meant

So different- yet so regular
But the two- are regular
Why must one choose
When presented with muse

For life is all too full
With choices- we must fill
Why couldn't I be greedy
And choose all that is needy

For I am but a pawn
In this land of dawn

Why but why is it one-th
When it could easily be both
A friend and lover
To give us both the power

FRIENDSHIP OR MORE

Sitting around, exchanging stories
Just like once in a while - and always,
This time around - something- felt different
The hearts and the eyes- acting different

The hearts beating- to their own rhythm
The eyes talking- their own idiom
As if the hearts are whispering
As if the eyes are replying

The bodies- inching closer together
To fulfill- this subconscious desire
The hearts rejoicing and beating faster
The eyes shining brighter and brighter

The mind takes over with its wisdom
Resist it! Resist it! He scream
This cannot be and will not
The friendship will suffer a lot

Hands joined together in harmony
Pulling each other more intensely
Into each other's arms we reprieve
Seeking some sort of a relief

Eyes staring at each other
Filled with lust and desire
Realizing- this cannot be!
Choosing a hug- to last eternity

ONE OF A KIND

A chest to lean on,
A shoulder to cry on,
Ears to listen, eyes to console,
A comforting touch, a lonely soul
For the reassurance that is needed
A rare find in this global world

A golden heart - comes shining in
To mend - a broken one within
Out of darkness, one emerges
Words of wisdom and healing touches

Spreading comfort - where one is needed
Creating hope - where despair has spread
Radiating love - where none exists
Mending the heart - with the broken strings

A rare find in this earth
Someone- with a golden heart
True to his feelings, true to his words
Loyalty and honesty define who he is

Search around for that special friend
For under a rare gem he will be found
Hang on to him with all you command
For he truly is- one of a kind

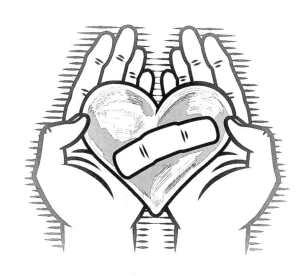

LOVE

BROKEN

Feeling lonely and distant
Full of sorrow and lament
Tears streaming forcefully
Like a stream rushing deeply

Broken up into a thousand thought
Trying to navigate throughout
Thoughts flowing with no direction
Like the wind blowing in every direction

Chest becoming tighter and tighter
Making every breath harder,
Heart bleeding from within
Blood flowing in its broken string

Trying to find a way out
With every beat that comes out
An arrow sharply penetrating
Deeper and deeper aiming,
Reaching the soul with its might
Breaking to pieces all that might

Tried as I can to find a justification
To no avail no rationalization
All the questions have been asked
All the wondering have stopped

With no answers in sight
I turn to life for a light:
Love! Is the answer
As it allows feeling further

It is what it is my dear weakling
For love is the reason for being,
Try as I might to avoid it all
There is no escaping it at all,

It is a gift from the heavens
To all beings on this earth,
To give resemblance to the almighty
Love - must conquer it all righty

DATES OF REGRETS

Strong in our belief and faith
Thinking our values can handleth,
With our trust and devotion- standing
A full on storm - weathering

So strong in our convictions
Yet - so weak in our desires
Holding on solidly to our values
Yet - so frail in lustful moments

Weak second when you least expect it
To test your will at odd moment
Thinking we are solid- but easily giving in
Discovering we are- but a weakling human

August fourth, January sixteenth
April ninth, October thirteenth,
Dates of excitement and pleasure
Followed by days of regrets and torture

Dates of turmoil and torment
Dates to never be forgotten,
Forever printed in the memory
The weak moments- will always haunt yee

Images so real and intense
Body aches with remorse
Feelings of sorrow and regret
Overtaking the soul and the spirit

Dates of regrets!!!
Life's hardest moments
Yet
The most teachable ones

UNABLE TO HATE

Friends for a long time
Intimate for a little time,
Thinking he was different
He will cherish and appreciate,
Doing things previously never done
Give up what you are for one.
Finding out he is like all the others
No less- but maybe worse,
Using the friendship as a guise
To build the intimacy piece,
Once things have progressed
More than the intimacy abandoned

Wanting so much to hate
Yet unable to hate,
For hate was a foreigner to me
So the hurt started consuming me
For love - was the only emotion learned
By the heart, soul, spirit, and mind

Lost in this contradiction
Tearing my insides in all direction,
Wanting to hate
Yet unable to hate,
What's one to do in this event
When hate was never felt

Lost- but not knowing what to do
Run- but not knowing where to go
I turn to life, an answer requesting
Only to find its own game- life's playing
Keeping him here, near, and there
as a teaser and a tormenter

Yelling, screaming, and crying
Answers and direction demanding,
A new revelation forthcoming
Shocking and jolting my being,
Not what's expected but what's given
For it is the reality of this human:
I was never taught to hate
I was never subjected to hate
I was never intended to hate
I was never meant- to feel hate

This revelation finally understanding
Reluctantly and forcibly accepting,
Stuck in this quandary
No other answer discovery,
Still - wanting to hate
Still - unable to hate

GRAVITY

Gravity, gravity, gravity
Where would I be without yee,
Although you keep me standing
Flying in the air preventing,
You might also be knowing
All other things affecting

The tension of that chemistry
That is strengthened by gravity,
It keeps on pulling and pulling
Until no longer standing,
For one could try to get away
From the pull run away,
Run, run to no aim
For the pull of gravity remain

The mind whispers nay
The heart screams yay
The will in a state of flight
The body tries its might
To run and pull away
Alas unable to get away

The pull of gravity remain

WHAT IS LOVE

Love, what is love?

Love -
The fire inside of us
The heart- it keeps it pumping
In every direction- spreading

Love -
The hope that controls us all
Spreading joy and happiness to all

Love -
The bread that nurtures the body
The water that cultivates the psyche

Love -
The scent of the mystical flowers
One can never ignore or forgets

Love -
The wind that helps the bird
Fly high into the vast sky and wild

Love -
The rays that shines in one's eyes
Providing light where none exists

Love –
The moonlight that shines our night
Providing lovers a space to reunite

Love –
The beauty of seeing nothing but color
Filling the world with beauty like no other

Love –
The breath of all beings
Eternal connection one must profess

Love –
The gentle touch that awakens the senses
The peace of mind that assures the senses

Love –
The beast that awakens us all
Life is beautiful, worth living, and vital

Where would one be without it all
No need to find out- love surround us all

WHAT WILL IT BE

What to do with a meeting possibility
A racing mind about this opportunity,
How to act with the first glance
Aim for a short hug - or a long embrace!

Filled with all the pleasuring emotions
Feeling all the passion and sensations,
Wanting, yearning, and craving
The one touch, that will be satisfying

Feeling every little wetness
Wanting more than just a kiss,
Tormented and anxious
Anguished and helpless

The question still remains
What will it be?

LOVE IS ETERNAL

Love is a forever rollercoaster
Love is living for another
Love is being all that you can
Love is doing all that you can
Love- is eternal

Eyes- that see only you
Hands- that touch only you
Heart- that beats only to you
Body- longing only for you
Love- is eternal

Lips- intertwined and encircled
Breath- collectively harmonized
Cheeks- lightly touching
Two bodies into one- moving
Love- is eternal

Feeling his envies
Fulfilling his desires
Celebrating his wishes
Living as one
Love- is eternal

One body,
One breath,
One heart-beat,
Transforming two- into one
                Love- is eternal

LOVE

It doesn't come knocking
                    It doesn't ask permission,

It doesn't wait for anyone
                    It doesn't wait discussing,

It breaks all the walls
                    And barges right in,

It hears no one
                    And listens to nothing,

It sees no one-
                    And looks straight ahead,

To the one and only holder

                    Of the key - to the heart that loves

LOVE IS BLIND

Love is blind
Love is strange
For one doesn't know
From where will it come

Wondering in life
Like all other creatures
Minding my business
For all I can

Suddenly there it comes
Unannounced and not requested
Barging in with no warning or consent
Taking control of all that I am

Taking control of my being
Overwhelming me and my feeling
Try as I might to shake it off
To no avail- for no one can

Love is blind in every way
It takes control of one's heart
With no mercy and no forgiveness
Instead with passion and compassion

Filled with sensations and emotions
Stirs up the sleepiness in you
As every sense is longing for something
And the heart pumps with delight
To a beat- of its own creation

Love is blind in every direction
Not knowing where to look,
Where to hide, or take cover
It will find you no matter what
Like your own shadow that shines

Take it in- without complaints
For it is a feeling like no other,
Breath it in- as it conquers all
For love is blind to it all

LOVE IS COMPLETE

A look, a whisper, a touch
A shiver, a tremble, an excitement
Love is described

One breath, one heart, one thought
Alive, refreshed, invigorated
Love is defined

A breath fills me up-
As his eyes meet mine,
A whisper crosses boundaries-
Trembling the heart all over,
Excitement fills the body-
As fingers touches the skin,
Thoughts of yearning imagination-
Rushes through me in all direction
Love takes over

Body to body,
Skin to skin,
Lips to lips,
Breath to breath,
Intertwined in complete harmony,
One completes the other
Love is complete

FIRE

Walking into the room
Searching through the swarm
Our eyes meet in an infinite stare
Locked in an indefinite glare

Reaching deeply into the soul
Without our will or control
Reading all feelings and thoughts
Exposing all our deep secrets

Your hands caressing my skin intensely
Reaching deeply and profoundly
Our bodies inching even closer
Forming mirror image of each other

Faces inching nearer and closer
Forcing them to ask for further
Lips moving, touching, and teasing
Souls get a shaking and a jolting

Senses attentive and prepared
Feeling weak and distracted
Trying to find meaning for it all
Yet anxious- about it all

Swallowing a knot in my throat
As it continues down the gut
Filling my insides with THAT feeling
Jolting me into a state of longing

Heavy breathing and deep sighs
Racing heart and sweating palms
More and more the body aches
Lips screaming for wetness

A fondle- the bosoms longing
Lust and desire bursting
Legs rapidly and firmly crossed
This progression hoping to end

Emotions high and uncontrolled
THIS feeling unable to end
Urging for a relief to come forth
I scream and let everything go-eth

There he comes with his valor
Fulfilling all my longing and more
Making my achiness travel
As his touch brings an arousal,

Bodies wrapped in one
Intertwined together like one
One discovering the other
One simultaneous move after another

A l-o-n-g s-l-o-w and final sigh
Brings me to a state of delight
Bosoms mesmerized and satisfied
Enjoyment rendering them tendered,

Heart leaping and dancing
Slow and controlled with every beating
Lips locked into a gentle kiss
As the body returns to a state of bliss

Content and in a state of ecstasy
Satisfying a dream and a fantasy
Lying there and wondering
How and where was the beginning

Search as I might in all direction
To no avail there is no explanation
Love's fire we will never depict
All we could do is yield to its might.

"It is we who nourish the Soul of the World, and the world we live in will be either better or worse, depending on whether we become better or worse. And that's where the power of love comes in. Because when we love, we always strive to become better than we are"

- Paulo Coelho, *The Alchemist*

Made in the USA
Middletown, DE
05 December 2017